D0853289

Four Young Women
POEMS

Edited and Introduced by
KENNETH REXROTH

Four Young Women

POEMS

BY JESSICA TARAHATA HAGEDORN,
ALICE KARLE, BARBARA SZERLIP
AND CAROL TINKER

McGRAW-HILL BOOK COMPANY
New York   St. Louis   San Francisco   Düsseldorf
London   Mexico   Sydney   Toronto

First Edition   123456789BPBP79876543

Library of Congress Cataloging in Publication Data
Rexroth, Kenneth, date   comp.
   Four young women.
   1. American poetry—20th century. I. Hagedorn,
Jessica Tarahata, 1949–   II. Title.
PS589.R48   811'.5'408   72-10091
ISBN 0-07-073844-0

Contents

v

vi

CAROL TINKER

Introduction

Is it necessary to make an apology for a new poetry
series? There are certainly enough of them around.
Trouble is it's hard to tell one from another, or one
book from another. If it's possible to make it so, and it
surely is, this one is going to be different.

In the first place one of its functions will be to
introduce relatively unpublished and genuinely young
poets. "Young poet" in the language of book reviewers
seems to mean somebody who doesn't rhyme. They
were referring to William Carlos Williams and Wallace
Stevens as young poets when both men were in their
fifties.

The great bulk of poetry published in even the
most radical series is conventional, with the conventions
of a past era. It is provincial, the product of seminars
in Creative Poetry dominated by the theories of the
long-bygone New Criticism and the examples of English
baroque verse and the American self-styled Reactionary
Generation. There is an established international idiom
of modern verse which was developed to handle the

situation of modern man. It certainly is not new. Baudelaire, Rimbaud, Mallarmé, Apollinaire—by the end of the First World War it had been perfected and internationalized. There are plenty of American poets who write this way. There are plenty of American poets aware of the vast spiritual crisis of our time and its reflection in the crisis of sensibility. Not because of the novelty of their style, but because of what they say, they still find it hard to get published.

As any teacher of "Creative Poetry" will tell you, the majority of students who write poetry are women and usually they write better than the men. After about the age of twenty-five they begin to disappear. What happens to them? The answer is apparent upon even the most cursory survey of literary magazines and small presses. They find it very hard indeed to get published. Many anthologies of genuinely young poets, many series of poetry booklets contain no females whatsoever. Perhaps it would be possible to make an effort to correct this imbalance.

Certain kinds of poetry by members of racial minorities in the United States find ready publication. A stereotype is growing up as rigid as that of the old minstrel show. Protest, revolt are fine, but black, brown and yellow people are human beings and live human lives with human problems and human glories and do something else besides protest even if that's all the guilty dominant race wants to hear. Then too, we should be able to look forward to a time when there will be a free flow of the vitalizing streams of tradition between Africa, the Orient, Indian and Latin America, and the poets of the United States, whatever their color.

It has often been said that poetry and music are the two pivots of the counter culture. The times are

changing—all over the world—and the output of poetry
that reflects that change is enormous. The best of it
should be made available in English while it is fresh.

It is fitting that the first volume of the series should
be titled *Four Young Women*. Among them they satisfy
most of the criteria I have just listed. They are all
actually young. They are women. They are good writers,
highly skilled in the use of their instruments, and they
write in a completely contemporary idiom. Their poems
if translated into any language would be readily
negotiable. Poets writing in Dutch or Tagalog would
recognize their kind of sensibility confronting their
situations. As a premium one of the four is in fact a
member of the Third World.

I, for one, have found illumination in the poems of
these four young women, and I am sure that others
will, too.

KENNETH REXROTH

Four Young Women

POEMS

The Death of Anna May Wong

JESSICA TARAHATA HAGEDORN

For Angela Davis

AUTOBIOGRAPHY PART ONE:
Manila to San Francisco

The pistol, yes.
Sheets of paper horizontally folded.
Men carry clocks
Into the room.
The pistol.
A letter to my father
Forgotten.
Voices from open windows
Do not break rules.
Two lips kiss.
The sun rises
On the other side of the continent.
Every morning . . .
A plate and spoon beside the pistol.
Raised to the temple,
Its body is not quite round,
Sleek gray stone in my hand . . . a cup
Of milk spills.
The pistol is pressed to the skull—
Open mouth
Like butterfly wings
Murmuring supplications
Instead
Another kiss

Voices repeat the rules
From open windows.
Each clock
Strikes a different time

In Spain
A gypsy servant named
Candles of the Sun
Dances
On your birthday
And you will never forget
Her smell
And her dwarf-lover
Who followed you
Into the mountains . . . asking you
To wear his shoes

That Gabriel
He's so polite
My dead brother who is buried. (My mother's
Hemorrhage is a lump in the grave)
That Gabriel
My brother; my uncle;
My father;
The dwarf:
Who carries a pistol
And wears rubber shoes

Your ankles
Are too frail
For these mountains
But you persist
In climbing them anyway
So you can say:

"I've seen the ruins
Of Guernica; in my hometown
There's even a nightclub named
Guernica."

4

Candles of the Sun
My sandlewood gypsy . . .

The pistol, the pistol,
Yes!

I live on the street
Of police ghosts and pimps . . .
The rebels who avenge them
Ask for money
And threaten to blow
My brains out.

The pistol, the black revolver
The nightmare
The swollen eye
The gun!
I will gun you down,
I will shoot you
I will kill you.
I will molest you
I will assault you
I will kiss your cunt
I will blow you up.
I will shoot! I will
Gun you down!
But not . . . but not . . . forever . . .
Not yet.

In China
A girl
Her coarse hair flies
In the afternoon wind
She is a genuine colony concubine

5

Who drinks tea
At exactly four-fifteen at the
Peninsula hotel (Oh yes, baby, in
a silk shantung-slit yellow-legged
fantasy)
An all Chinese (that is to say grease
and dandruff orchestra)
Plays Mantovani
and Monteverdi and George Gershwin

There is a border
One cannot cross
Although the guards are not visible.
George Gershwin
Mantovani and Monteverdi
Have not ceased
Being British
In Kowloon
But across territory lines
The guards remain
Invisible.

Two magazines
A cigarette-filled abalone shell.
The invisible weapon.
Down the street
Sleeps the wife
Of a revolutionary.
Avenge them all,
On behalf of Chrysler-Pontiacs!
There are twenty-four tactics
According to the pamphlet.
The inevitable result

Is the inevitable electronic solution.
Oh, lies! Lies! Lies!
I am neither or either.
Perpetrator, traitor, user of soap!
Lies! So thin
So metallic, so invisible!
Police shadows
On ghost motorcycles
Patrol the streets. It is too late—
I am up before dusk
Watching the sunset ... It is too soon—

In Asia
One dies slowly
Fanning off the heat
With a stiff palm leaf.
I love you, Garcia-Villa
You are not the only one
Who is going to die
In the city
Wearing velvet slippers
And a patched red shirt

You are a man
In between airplanes
Semi-retired, a not-so notorious
Professor of the word

A torpid university dream.

In Asia
One dies too slowly
Without weapons ...

In America
The smell of death pervades
Among its women
In department stores . . .
They linger, tubercular sparrows
With bony throats and sooty lashes
Peering elegantly
From behind diamond-clear counters.

My country of old women!

My sweet nicotine-tooth
Prostitute . . .

Give me a receipt
For your time.

1968

AUTOBIOGRAPHY PART TWO:
Rock and Roll

We boogied when I was eight
I had just learned to dance
Carl Perkins sang "Matchbox"
And I hated him

But anything was better
Than Bill Haley or Frankie Laine
Until Elvis and Little Richard;

I wanted them so much
I would've known how to fuck them then
In joyous appreciation

When I was ten
It was Etta James
I didn't know what she looked like,
If she were male or female

I worried about my odor
When I did the slowdrag
And the guys had their
Sideways erections
To Etta James

And then
Chubby Checker and Joey Dee
Red shirts stained with sweat

Tight white toreador pants

9

American tennis shoes—

In 1960 Elvis was a drag
Harry Belafonte gave a concert
At the Coliseum
The older chicks dug him.
(He wore a beautiful tangerine
Shirt open at the throat)

Fabian was doing his tiger
We posed for a photograph
Together
Cost me three pesos
And an autographed lace
Handkerchief

1962 and Philadelphia Italians
Fabian Frankie Avalon Dion and the Belmonts
With poufed blond hair

I was in Hongkong
Buying Bobby Vee records
And then Tokyo
Buying Paul Anka
"Live at the Copacabana"

San Francisco
Was a gray dream
A gray meat market harbor

I thought it was Chicago

My mother cried
A lot then

Her face was gray

The Four Seasons were very big
For some reason
I hated them

They weren't even
A good shuck.

My first weeks in
San Francisco and I was
Surrounded by faggots;
Lovely gilt-frame
Antique faggots:
My uncles my mothers
My dubious friends—

Bill Haley was dead
Bobby Vee was dead
Little Richard in some church

Yes, yes Little Anthony
Was very big then . . .

I will never forget him.

March, 1969
Dedicated to the poet
Victor Hernandez Cruz.

THE DEATH OF ANNA MAY WONG

My mother is very beautiful
And not yet old.
A Twin,
Color of two continents:

I stroll through Irish tenderloin
Nightmare doors—drunks spill out
Saloon alleys falling asleep
At my feet . . .

My mother wears a beaded
Mandarin coat:
In the dryness
Of San Diego's mediterranean parody
I see your ghost, Belen
As you clean up
After your sweet señora's

mierda

Jazz,
Don't do me like that.
Mambo,
Don't do me like that.
Samba, calypso, funk and
Boogie
Don't cut me up like that

Move my gut so high up
Inside my throat
I can only strangle you
To keep from crying . . .

My mother serves crêpes suzettes
With a smile
And a puma
Slithers down
                19th street and Valencia
Gabriel o.d.'s on reds
As we dance together

Dorothy Lamour undrapes
Her sarong
And Bing Crosby ignores
The mierda.

My mother's lavender lips
Stretch in a slow smile.
And beneath
The night's cartoon sky
Cold with rain
                Miss Alice Coltrane
Kills the pain
And I know
I can't go home again.
1971

BIRTHDAY POEM FOR GREGORY REEVES

The unicorn flies
                    over my head
and the toucan
                    chinguela
                              (little fucker)
nibbles
        on a child's hand
                          held tightly
in its beak
The table is scattered with dreams
                    a dead chrysanthemum
                                          dangles
                                                    over
a cup of cold tea
                    baby snakes
                                slither
                                        among paper stars
cut-out valentines
                    and
                        crystal gloves
A butterfly asleep
                    on a windowpane
shattered
        by
            ivory cocaine
                          spoons
                                    and metallic triangles
                                                    bells
        and untouched green apples

14

A wax mushroom
                    my dress
                              uncovered pear breast
                              uncovered heart
turquoise Aztec necklace
                    and
                              the Virgin Mary's
        Immaculate Conception smiles
                              at me
His pink hand
              in the toucan's beak
                              unbloody
                                        and cold
                        as tea
The clock   surpasses time
            a gift
                    from a hermaphrodite
who
      works as a dancer
                    in North Beach
and
      outside
              my mind's eye
The moon turns white
                    and a house
                                floats
          in
              the sky
(the toucan, little fucker
              swallows Jesus Christ)

1971

15

FILIPINO BOOGIE

Under a ceiling high Christmas tree
I pose
        in my Japanese kimono
My mother hands me
                        a Dale Evans cowgirl skirt
and
      baby cowgirl boots

Mommy and daddy split
No one else is home

I take some rusty scissors
                        and cut the skirt up
        in
            little pieces

(don't give me no bullshit fringe,
 Mama)

Mommy and daddy split
No one else is home

    I take my baby cowgirl boots
                        and flush them
                                    down
                            the
                                    toilet

(don't hand me no bullshit fringe,
 Papa)

I seen the Indian Fighter
Too many times

16

                    dug on Sitting Bull
                                before Donald Duck

In my infant dream

These warriors weaved a magic spell

            more blessed than Tinker Bell

(Kirk Douglas rubs his chin
 and slays Minehaha by the campfire)

Mommy and daddy split
There ain't no one else home

                    I climb a mango tree
                            and wait for Mohawk drums
(Mama—World War II
 is over . . . why you cryin'?)

Is this San Francisco?
Is this San Francisco?
Is this Amerika?

buy me Nestle's Crunch
            buy me Pepsi in a can

Ladies' Home Journal
            and Bonanza

I seen Little Joe in Tokyo
I seen Little Joe in Manila
I seen Laramie in Hongkong
I seen Yul Brynner in San Diego
and the bloated ghost
                    of Desi Arnaz
dancing
        in Tijuana

17

Rip-off synthetic ivory
                    to send
                            the natives
        back home

and
            North Beach boredom
                                escapes
                                        the barber shops

on Kearney street
                    where
                            they spit out
                                        red tobacco

                                patiently
            waiting
                    in 1930's suits

and in another dream

                        I climb a mango tree
and Saturday
            afternoon
                    Jack Palance
                                bazookas

                                the krauts
            and
                the YELLOW PERIL
                            bombs
                                    Pearl Harbor

1971

18

DREAM WAR

Nieves
     You are snow
with flaming red hair
You
     are the woman
they dragged
       in the streets of Hongkong
Nieves
     You are the shame of guerillas
who execute you
       in the afternoon heat
of Hongkong
The shadow of mandrills
     and weeping Portuguese mothers
who watched you die
      from
       their balconies
Your ghost
     visits occasionally
      in
       its fat pallor
with the perfume
     of dogpiss
      in
       your hair.

1970

LOVE POEM FROM AN UNFAITHFUL LADY

A toe
With amorphous mountain
On its back
Becomes another poem
Innumerable and vast
Without my mentioning
It would be
The purest statement of love
And pain.
         Today buffalo bill
And I (as is in childhood again)
Walked the neighborhood streets
Apart from the old gang
(yes, we are all friends)
You
Are more buffalo bill
Than any of them
Because it's a secret even
From you,   an innocent cowboy
In my belly valley.
Come in my room (anyway, even through
my door)
My last gazelle
Before dying:
Shut us out of the rain
Drink some beer and watch pinhead t.v.
(unbelievable Beckett)   with me

It sure is nice
        to be here
                Yes
                    it
                    sure
                        is

1969

ROCK AND ROLL

 I declare
That this is
A baby machine
That will tell us
When the time comes
Exactly how we begin
Not unlike
The unbending of zoo bars
By
Orangutans.

July, 1969

THE BLUE SWAN CAFE

I believe I will die young
The boy said to me
His moustache glistening
In the blue darkness

He handed me a dish
Of sweet petit fours
Quite stale by then
(The middle of the week)

His lover
owned the cafe; fortyish
Already

A shrivelled black man
Also with a moustache
As if painted across his mouth

To exclaim a kiss
more readily.

Loving terribly
Like some desperate woman
He hovered ominously
Near his green-eyed sweet-as-pastry
Young with an unfortunate
Fat ass

But skinny still all in all

Not yet twenty
Younger than me
He wants to die
Both of them play the part
Badly

Slamming cakes and
Sandwiches (delicately embedded
in pale lettuce like the young
fluttering eyes as only they know
how to do it) on tables
Covered with rotting flower petals

Already
There are too many pimples
On his pristine face
His mouth
Gulps down every crumb
Of stolen pink Renoir meringue
That his lover
Leaves for him behind
the counter, one of his many gifts
For greedy young men.

In the end of night I glance
At each face inside the cafe
Eyes half-closed
In the stupor
Of boredom;

How should they die
Together

If not to take us
With them?

August, 1969

2

  broken cups:
           do not forget.
tomorrow i shall re-examine
          the camera.
A

  woman screams:
           death is delightful.
my spool of film
        is backward.
2

  broken cups:
         the damage is irreparable,
As in a poem.

1968

FILLMORE STREET POEMS: August, 1967.

1.

Into the deepest mornings
Strange harmonious cries are sung
By roving leopards
Who shatter windows   and minds
Exalting the cunts
Of fresh young girls

2.

Sweet soft face
Bloated and defiled
By morticians and priests:
There are violent celebrations
In the street

3.

The Chinaman knows it all
Keeps secrets locked up
Inside a vintage cash register

4.

At the corner
One glimpses
Occasional dreams
Hung-out to dry by twenty-five-year-old women
Whose backs are stooped.
They have looked away
From me before
And will again (having understood what I wasted)

27

5.

GOLDSTEIN'S—GOLDFARB'S—WE BUY AND SELL
Blond wigs and
Hard round asses   strutting
Before the dull gold eyes of men
Waiting to call out truth
To strangers
         BUT

6.

The Chinaman has truth
Locked up
In his cash register too

7.

Gunfire spit
In the distance
The young fresh girls
Have left the street
The construction zone
Will resound tomorrow
It doesn't make a difference
Who died
        yesterday

They have looked away
From us before
But not again.

THE FUNDAMENTAL MAN

 Who sees the stranger
Grasp
To maintain his balance
On a transcontinental bus
Bound for New York

Where nothing's justified to him
Squatting in a bathtub
Of bathbubbles and lice

Denouncing all in retrospect.

Praying to Jesus interim
On the transcontinental bus
Bound for New York

Delicately nibbling
Female flower petals
Burnt and pornographic

O lust's salvation!

(The stranger too, grows old,
remembering New York)

1965

POEM FOR RENE CREVEL

 I am pretending
To listen to the
Battered radio
      cigarette involuntarily
Stuck between cord
And plug
Electrically nubilous

You have conjugated
Godliness
Ochroid face
      smashed
Between cord
And plug
Ochroid image swallowing
Young plum breasts
Wet and purple

But there's contradiction
Within my belly
Too,   fine urges
Which shoot dully
        and
Penetrate my backbone
In violent dreams.

In the city's vulgar
Afternoon, what's the use
Of death?
We become iatric poets,
You and I

1965

A PLASTER AND PLEXIGLAS CREATION

 With dusty beams
Of light magnifying
Fantasies
Voices penetrating
The impenetrable

My unseen eye peers
Through delicate
Substances that blind
All others

Who anyway stand in line
And wait

Namedropping ("I remember
Marcel Duchamp") And
Feeling each other
Anxiously

Bored; wearing common
Red dresses (it is a cruelty
to misunderstand the plexiglas)
Kissing

Museum doors

And copulating before
Indifferent curators

32

So that I am alone
And almost abandoned at
The exhibit

Writing nonsensical letters
And forgetting
That it's been
A long time

Since the last war.

1965

LETTER TO RAFAEL: 1966

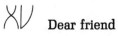 Dear friend
                  and stalwart gazelle
        whom I haven't   heard from
                        in just about a year:
        the time has come
        for me to say
        I've reached the end

        How's your red MG
        and your bitter father
        with a moustache
                        and your mother
        Who
        flushes your dreams
                        down
                                the
                                        toilet
        and your girlfriends
        who were always blonde
        and somewhat fat

        How was Munich
        and Copenhagen
        and the noisy smiles of soldiers

        You were always fighting me

        Thank you for your prompt replies
        I always did like you   even when
        34

I could no longer answer hasty questions
mailed
        from places   only   you
                        could know.

FOR BRUCE WHO'S ON SMACK: May 31, 1967

 In February
sometime
you gave me
an iris stalk

Its petals
tasted like
the pale wax
            blueness
of
your eyes

There was
a 16-year-old princess
in the room
who faked
a Cockney accent
            (her dress covered
            soft plump legs)
When you laid
your head
            down
and tried
not to touch me

I would have never
thought of you now

Someplace
36

without her giggling
and aborting babies
casually
      without a shrug
of her round shoulders
to soothe you

Where you sleep
this morning
      without
           dreams

EPIC EULOGY FOR BOY AND GIRL WHO ALMOST KILLED EACH OTHER WITH ASPIRIN FOR LOVE AND HOMOSEXUALITY AND PREGNANCY'S SAKE

XVII

(What if tomorrow
we were dead
our hands together
our bodies straining on the bed,
for us, for boredom,
our games have ended)

I offer you a bunch
                    of walt disney flowers
because I love you still . . . excuse

my mediocrity
                but I've tried other things before

They never worked on you.
            She was meaningless at 17
            Somewhat resembling an anemic rabbit
            But beautiful   when her hair
            Fell loose

            Couldn't you see her all blown up?

            So was he, meaningless and pale
            Except that he was 16 and obsessed
            With his father
            And unobtrusive leftist pocketbooks.
            He clutched them weakly
            Riding buses at odd hours
                            of the day

                and night
                        talking to young boys

                Even younger than he.
And I recall them
                        now
                                in haste
                                        in goodwill
                                                in love
You're a hard one to please; not even

Asmodeus helped. He only succeeded in scaring me

to death (almost to death) until I finally got the message.

Downtown's bearable
                        when you're stoned
So's walt disney
                        So take my soggy bunch of flowers

And kiss my frail female wrists
                        like they do in the movies.
It's been
        too long a time
                        without
                                you

A SCRIPT: Beauty is the beginning of terror ...

1. The sea.
2. The disappearance of the sun.
3. My love is red like blood.
4. The Sky.
5. My eye.
6. That monster, sleep, is hungry.
7. Young girls' faces.
8. White statues.
9. My love is red like blood.
10. Or I would die, the black revolver embracing me.

1968

Canto de Nada/Para ti, M'wandishi

her name is nada
daughter of ainu and t'boli
igorot and sioux
sister to inca and zulu

born from the mouth of a tree
the lullaby of joe loco
and mongo
turquoise eye
the lullaby of pattie labelle
and the bluebells
flowers of her smile
the strut   the style

she is the punk
the dancing girl
the brand new bag
purple and red
the brand new bag
the sweetness
the lullaby of herself
the riff of a biwa
the daughter of a sorceress
the gong
the dragon lady's baby

she is the punk
the dancing girl

la cucaracha   who can even
get up from her own o.d.

every night the color
of her hair
she is the song
soul sister number one
the brand new bag
her jewels are as loud
as her love

her name is nada
mother to rashid
koumiko   carmen miranda
ylang-ylang   ruby delicious
she is the cocaine princess
with the hundred dollar nose
gettin higher because she got
to aim for the stars

she is the star
she is the city
flaunting sequins
and butterflies
she is peru   mindanao
shanghai

the divine virgin
waitin for a trick
on the borderline
between emeryville
and oakland

at noon on sunday
at noon on monday
at noon   hail mary
full of grace

she is nada   all music
she is nothing   all music
she is the punk   all music
the dancing girl   all music

she is nada   nothing
she is the real thing

and in her womb
one could sleep
                    for
                        days

February, 1972.

ALICE

KARLE

Liebfraumilch

Bavaria
Market Einerstein
red home tops
green grass
simple churches
natural warm september Christmas
visit

"They are still vacationing
But you stay with us"
Hands that touch
faces that teach
Eachother
"Here is the church"

'I am a man of the honey'
said the preacher, but never said
        'the Preacher of Market Einerstein'
to a hitchhiker in Athens
'I am a man of the honey'

"They are still vacationing
He is the preacher
You know
His mouth is the comb
He speaks bees
But we make
for ourselves
the honey"

Snowmountains
way to Aspen
pines dark
Closer sun yellows and red
the blood clays range through mountain
The smaller trees in winter—graygreen with brown
their bones
Like the posts of old fence bits
White cow   inside

Orange truck
between snow and night
(Shows)
Found
friends, their home
Coincidence comes
a collection of nuclei
The heat of laughter
Laughter of heat

SUICIDE

You fell like silk slipping through itself
So quickly
The part between breaths should be
Easy
This part that only found a scratched out mirror
Both sides unknown

    A clam cellar locked safe
    Encloses darkness in fear
    I look out from the keyhole
    but the inside is not copper or reason
    or time
    And coincidence does not come

The sun is orange
Half a lung at daybreak
The part between breaths
Heavy not easy
Eyelashes like butterfly hairs too close to the fire
Fall   wings broken in smoke

The other lung did not fill
You fell
Quickly
Silk
Slipping
through itself

to Shannon and Kenneths

 Morning sparrow
freckled with sun
The blow fish rises
Inhale

Morning bread
Made with seeds
The blow fish rises
With full eyes

sideman   how many edges fill?
gray-tan
sideman
Heart from leandart
bloodbank of the water
sideman
sideman
tide shore salt liquid fingers
                touch, turn
what is left
what is
surely, shore
bloodbanks
sideman
gray-tan
sideman
sideman

thickskin orange
peels free
slips free touched into the night like a girl into the night
thickskin orange
nourishes dark volcano's heart
Heart from leandart
bloodbank at Pompeii
from the dark
what is left
sideman fills the edges??
how many,   sideman

51

"Darkness"
—to John Wilson

The sun fits eyes in bluemountain
Light washes out
ocean rocks   mounds
       rounded worn breasts

The night though is an echo
Canyon's red rocks fire   voice
gun   Echo cringe
fire's stillen dropped clay

The sun fits eyes in bluemountain
Light washes out the pain
      like the origin of thalidomide
And I forget eroding heads
       falling under wet beds

Elizabeth

I sat staring at an anthill for almost forever
Someone had turned the music down so low I could not hear
And I watched ants carrying broken fragments of sand
   down into and through a tiny
   hole as they disappeared
   Into their funnel
   home below

My home
My home is purple
The blues separated
My home is red but I do not want to die
I know the anthill is a funnel grave
Yet I watch for almost forever separate my breath
   pour my heartbeats
   one fraction to each ant
Fracture each one through the fine point of music and non music
   the balance almost dissolved
   through each other

And my heart's bloodless tears

But inside this numb
Fire rubbing against itself
Spreading to my eyes

And the anthill melted flat like an album
And the blues and red spinning into each other
I could hear them

53

Spring trees grow heavy
Leaves, milk   soon mother
Bones   glow with the elements
        from rich dirt
Frame heavy: her home
Leaves: little wombs
        half egg smiles

IX
The days and nights of the river
Line heavy
Like coincidence is light
The river has banks
Does chance have edges

Figouras, Figouras, Figouras
Figs grow for free in the mountains
This train is not drunken like the poor Spanish trains
This train is going to France where
                    Johnny's-Delicatessen-
                    Ash-Wine
                    And Bob Dylan may be
                    after only another flood

And Before,
Before is the beauty of the river

I smile a heavy-eyed sleepy smile
Thinking of you and me and this morning
When the river is very beautiful after too

A delicate snowflake in the middle of the desert
How long will its waters flow each way
Here there are many edges to ants and
Flood and day and night
Light and heavy and Figouras
Melt together in this morning

The lines in your hand
And the lines in my hand
Look as different as rivers
We place our hands together
And let them wash

I sit with my hands in the river
Where have they gone without me
The Indian lady too quickly walks by
She looks for her child
The valley points four ways to the reservation
Her child is dead

A Play

XI The quiet
The quiet
The quiet kisses like the one hand claps
The quiet
The quiet
The sound of the sea sleeping with me

My room
My room grows more yellow yellow grows purple
purple flowers
Uncompleted like this

The quiet is room
The sea is sun
The sun is yellow
This will always be young

The purple hand is less and more than That
The clap
The quiet

The room is one brown color
But the brown bricks spell Eve
I did not know the cold moon is red
Until I saw it rise

The place may soon change
Like anything carried to extremes

The silence will know where they meet
In the prism colors of clear water
we can see their lips press eachother

XIII   Steps   Steps
Spaces   inbetween   steps
In-between   steps, steps
Spaces.

Closeness   comes to faces
A mountain and an ocean
Inbetween : space
The silver lillie graces
The barren Mexico desert—
The spaces
The spaces
Between
Faces
Step
About.   "Farewell
Forward."
Step
Forward.   "Farewell."
Step   Step
The spaces inbetween
The glow.   Product of
No direction
No About
Or Fro
The radiant Lillie
Of the Empty Spaces
Grows.

An Epic
(with Renaissance Flute)

Part
1

We went in the Green Grasshopper

Part
2

The young queen was Elizabeth
The old queen was Ezmeralda

Part
3

Warning!
There are only three mystics here
Get your fortune told in convolutionary reflections
Before the line goes to . . .
the next booth

Part
4
(Play)

And Elizabeth fell in love
                with the tree of Springtime
                who slew the long nosed
                wicked Winter
                in front of everybody

And she, envining Spring Tree
                    dubbed him her May Night
                    in front of everybody

Part
5

There were only three mystics
And there was a witch and
                    also a retired witch

But we picked the I CHING
And put our yarrow sticks in the Green Grasshopper
                    to bring them home later

Part
6

We mazed through the purple velvet ladies
And tunic tighted gentlemen
And some carried Ezmeralda in pomposity
                    forth in procession
And we looked at the velvet and
                    tunic stores that were
                    planted in pottery
                    in a stained glass greenhouse
That was etched in the Soul Food Stand

Part
7

Enveloping the air is Ougluup
          the mystoput
     of the three mystics

                    the witches
                    and the I CHING
Ougluup
Is soft while you play with it and keep it moving
And is hard when you break it

Part
8

I heard the wind sing that
                    the recipe for Ougluup
                    is very simple

Part
9

In back of our exit was Ezmeralda
                              panting and bloated
Wanting someone to carry her forth in procession
                              to her car
We drove the Green Grasshopper
                              to the grass by the water
We dove in the cool
We feasted
And then night to dream of it all

EARTHQUAKE

The hawk's nose
Crows
Offbeat hearts
     only knowing
     the owl
The owl
The owl
Who hoots the only
     emptyness
In blank paper
The hawk's nose
Crows

But you will   be standing
with ears   broken like
symmetrical   wishbone halfs

The street
Clear and empty
Veed in the middle
The fault
Has swallowed everyone

XVI Light floats through the edges
Light like cobweb dust
pulling up its tiny hairs around
an empty center

The window has been broken
Its veins and arteries
show the spider's tracks
I am in awe of
the nonmeaning

XVII Some come in the window
Is it nothing next to the sea
There, root hairs in my wine
I find your rolling like a sun tongue
The mouth is dark

In San Francisco,
Terry has the tank of nitrous oxide—
Laughter without hairs—like prison
In San Francisco
Dreams of Attica
Jessica writes a poem, "Angel Divino,
                        Angel Soledad"

And does not even realize—
like the quiet

Kenneth swims in Japan lagoon
Later orange kimono
sits reading aloud like the sun

A dark circle around the eyes
Joe, very hungry but afraid of smoke
Sits   with his other head
Slit   from the belly soft and up
and his eyes
65

where the tides retreat for a while
too dry to cry

I
In calf morning

Lew Welch
Ate by Bronze Turkey Buzzard
The female he saved
He is the young
Bird   he has wings
"Angel Divino" does not rhyme below trees
The rains came
after the headache
Bottle of dark cloud broke

TO LEW WELCH
two and a half years you and friend sing for us in these caves . .
                                                            still . .

First Bird Crest
Not Eagle
Mission Canyon
Red   underground
The caves paint higher
              under the mountain
Sand paint
Caves
Man with key now flown away
Key behind
Bronze Buzzard dropped
        to your heart

Song of Circles

 My tree   my tree
where do you go
You go in circles
you talk
hairs in your line
line of your toe
toe in your hand

Sometimes comes out in ripples
Some light hands   call   breaths
Before this stone
the pit curls it's feather edges

Mother of willow
Father of rainbow
baby of rain

catch the sun
hold the moon

Can you come inside
That is, your rainbow
My lips
my lips   are sticky
Only a little
only a little water
67

my meadow has purple flowers,
tastes of honey

year
slinky
ice-cream-cone
hula hoop

The rice paper tree
leaves leaves almost every day
The tree sees he, frog sit
wake up to chant like Bodi
eat drone   for breakfast
Queen comes out and gives frog all her honey

year
slinky
ice-cream-cone
hula hoop

Drone takes one   double scoop with nuts
Pretty cocky bee   bee
too pooped to hula
too fat to hoop
sleeps in cone

Can you come to the leaves
In moon they are still full
                 still green
Can you come   this is new
68

Mother of willow
Father of rainbow
Baby of rain

catch the sun
hold the moon

Invisible Beasts

BARBARA
SZERLIP

your body is a wasteland
your eyes a desert

there is
an emptiness that comes
round, perfect

after bits of time
and landscape have dissolved
in
their irrelevancies

and we walk away
from pieces of ourselves
as simply as
leaving a room
behind a closing door

there is sand in your hair
as you let go the knob
and disappear
down so many hallways

Note To A Hitchiker Who Stayed For One Day
for Fernando

to resort
to the bastard medium of words
as to a religion—
what is left
when the meal is finished
and we build our house
from the scraps and bones

across these distances
the eyes are useless
and the small
subtle gestures wasted.
time becomes a matter
of just so many postage stamps

>   I saw your face, I saw it
>   change into an old man
>   I saw him
>   watching me

to resort
as to imagination
as to a compass
or to the sea
the directions sought
have no direction.
we cling to something
and it leads us
like a wife's body

74

"Bagdad," you asked
of the old bedhouin.
he searched the land distorted
by heat, white, flat,
with no rock or plant to break
its skin.
the place he offered
with such certainty you
could not distinguish
from anything else
in your life. direction is
where you find it.
"Bagdad," he said.

Nothing of Innocence

it is not words but the lack
of them.
I cause pain I am hollow
I am
not.

for Pinter words said
less than silence
but here the quiet
cannot
even whisper.

death I am even
less useful than
the Drake Hotel he said:
there
but not there.
in Philadelphia I sit
drawing monologues of roofs
and chimneys
in deaf air.

in the causing of pain
there is
a loss, a corruption
that makes known the places
that came before.

like a virgin aware
of her virginity only
at the moment of loss
the innocent know nothing
of innocence.

Who Will Finally Say

who will finally say
I am all heaven all hell
who will immortalize names
in obscene diaries, preserve them
tacked from the killing jar

do not sell your death to me
like some fragile antique complete with explanations
who ever told you I could heal
the lepers with a touch

all those sheets with their
cryptic scrawlings, descriptions
of my pyre-death that you plot
with a craftsman's eye
and how the body goes up in flames
before they get to light the fire

you say
I engineer against your innocence
that I am Delphic sibyl with goat dance visions
the beautiful junky of your lust
alchemist of your insomnia
it is some other woman with this face, these hands
her image haunts you
like peacock feather eyes

I am no plague no manna
the doors were not marked with blood
because of me . . .

you begin to bore me with your pain

there is no dark cathedral of trophies
with velvet hooks, crutches
holding up vulnerable smiles
the endless halls, the barrels
of mutilated wings, all this a part
of your invention, search
for the perfect, impossible muse
whose body of nets would tangle your sleep
in wet, primeval visions

The End of Something

why the call
for elaborate ritual
why the need
the unsubtle gesture
does complexity make it
simpler, keep it
further from anything
we can feel or know as real

the returning
of shirts the final
account the balancing
of the books

with your beauty I am
as uninvolved
as with telephones & river
beds. in that I am
somehow the first
of all your women

Four Short Poems

The poet is a hunter of invisible beasts that die
in captivity. The bars must be far enough apart as
to be out of visual range, that is, wide enough for
them to pass through. With patience, they can sometimes be trained to eat out of his hand.

Lines Upon Waking

see what you like
see what you like
about the sun who'll baptize you
about the moon who won't talk back

Beehive

the city.
the dance.

No Hay Olvido

like the light reaching us
from stars
dead a thousand years
the necropolis called memory
seeks recognition

59:Huan/Dispersion
for J., upon departure

you are bored with the waiting
going is interminable until one begins it
you call; wires suspend us
telephone poles break the sky
like so many cruxifictions

think of traveling, the properties
of things
Gunga Dar at the ashram in Quebec
whose name was the Ganges, the holy
young disciple, the reformed cocaine addict
think of crewcuts in Palm Beach
      what kingdom is this?   by what do you measure?
think of the fags in Provincetown & 30th Street Station
think of pigeons, how they are the same everywhere
notice the moon, how it fills and empties
notice the tides, when they empty and fill
Dispersion.   Success.
think of Orion in summer
when he's not available

collect the images, store them for winter:
piles of coral bones
bales of greased wool for spinning
the leather cup, the intricate look

remember when they ask
the important things
are human dignity and the element of mystery

82

tell them I said that. It is the legacy
I meant for you

It furthers one to cross the great water.
remember Heraclitus: be sure to notice
which foot touched which river
learn to dispel
the illusionary quality of travel only
by the body's knowledge
of that night's bed
then forget the lesson

Perseverance furthers.

This Place

I envy the solitude you
learned from me
I am jealous of the teacher
that I was for you

what I gave away were burdens I
could no longer carry
I wanted to be weak but you gave me wings
strapped them to my shoulders

in glorifying everything you've robbed me
of even the solitude
there are only the tired symbols left
occupying the body like a tenement for rent

o let us celebrate
our arrival to this place
burn fat candles hissing like cats
praise it with a song we have composed
for the occasion

and I am left like the parasite's vessel
like the mole, soft dumb and blind
moving through darkness

of all the moments
which was the moment of salt
when did sleep become weighted, the lids sewn shut
my stone tongue my stone shoes
the silence filling us
like water in an empty room

Ambassador's Daughter

where are we now where is the hope
left to ripen on the sills where
are the poems scrawled on train schedules in brown ink
the jars of colored stones
where are the letters that followed me everywhere
your letters asking what is freedom

I never understood what blackmailed your fear
where are the young men with their cheap cologne
did you really think that loneliness
                              would lead you into ecstasy

what of your virtue that you guarded like a grail
then gave away to a drunken stranger
your alter of sacrifices your highway shrine your house
where no one lived

we were young we said all the right things
how the city was a heartbeat
we put coins in the tin cup of the blind subway beggar
who sang Battle Hymn of the Republic
                              against the railway's scream

how is your father who hated you
                              for what you could not control
who gave you his name and threw away the key
you stood there while he marked your forehead
with the blood of dwarves you stood there and took it
and let it sink down to the valley of your bones

86

were you Demosthenes then
was it only a mouthful of stones that stopped you

and your dead forbidden brother
that heap of dust scuttling across the floor

then you moved to a higher country
higher walls the broken glass
wind chimes
                a cook with long greased braids a sunken tub
two chauffeurs and gypsies in the barranca two dogs
a cat and sleep late on sunday
jealousy was the education I had chosen then
you never understood my penny arcade wisdom
the camembert breakfasts, the matching shoes
the patio where each afternoon at four
you sipped the thin air like a medicine

you'd think we'd know the Present when it came
you'd think we'd stop the worship
                                of photographs and wine corks
and that Ignorance just this once would not enter
like a favorite son into his father's house

are you happy now with your balding lawyer husband
your sculptured life and your father's blessing
what have you learned
and will you teach me

Breech
for Debra, born October 1952

are you among the animals whose secret names
the human mouth is unable to pronounce?

do you teach a lesson
whose language we are not ready for?
are you a voice
equal to the silence that surrounds us?

I would build a strange church
in which you are the altar

twisted in the womb
your mind was quilted like a landscape
rows of arthritic fingers piecing the design
mountains. rivers.

among us
unfinished.
your child's face
woman's body and old man's walk

another time there would have been edges
wood stone metal
to heal you for salvation
a miller to grind your bones
for the passover cake
your blood for pudding
the flesh in layers between coarse salt

my childhood has spent its long days writing this.
my sister, they say I am an only child.
they are fearful of the cripple's wisdom.

is there no one else in the family
to take care of the tree
to bear children like this season's oak
prolific against the oncoming, heavy winter?
is it your silence that sounds
like the bones of my unborn children growing?

The Crossing

> Majorca has no character,
> but it has good light for painting. —Joan Miro

XI

1.

the starter hunched
at the blocks quivers with the whole race
inside him
the sprinter merely runs

2.

ancient stone fences separating nothing
from nothing
fish nets being mended in the square
melons suspended by ropes to ripen
(in the melon grower's house there were stacks
 like pyramids in corners)
your laughter breaking the air like a church
and on the road to Manacor cactus pears
the size of a child's fist
an entire country speaking the language
of a dead, lisping monarch

3.

the intensity of the motion of the pebble is
that it *cannot ever* move

4.

you never understood my reasons for leaving
five days of travel the crossing the crossing

when sleep finally came it was
of desecrated houses
cattle lying dead their mouths gaped open

90

this place
this dream
place
once left will be gone
in all ways but
memory
which is no guide

should I take
the advice I once gave
in a poem to
judge and remember by
each night's
bed

there is at
sundown
an old woman and
her daughter
by the square in front
of the drugstore who sits
each evening
roasting corn to sell
and you ask for todo
todo
and she takes a cob
on a wooden stick
spreads it hot
with fresh lime mayonnaise

91

grated cheese chili
powder and all for two
pesos you can walk
the street with your prize

and by that
miracle
will I hold on
to where I am to where
I have been

Icarus To His Father
> Icarus. Such doomed attempts
> are necessary.—John Fowles

XIII   What I have of wisdom
is yours
what knowledge acquired is a branch
from your tree of branches

my face
its calligraphy memorized
is no longer mine
my fingers my lips
gone
the gestures the
words have lost themselves
in echo
language is worn
like new clothing stiff
and odd to walk in

heaven and hell
are our own creations
bondage also is as we see it

what is there for me here
you have created the axe for chopping
and the saw
with arms & legs you transformed the xoana
from childish mounds to the temple's gods
and in your exile devised this hieroglyphic house
this labyrinth for the queen's mutant son
what remains except departure

93

these walls begin to scrape the skin by layers
meanwhile Minos considers a new tax
the wine harvest has turned to vinegar
today in Athens what do they whisper in the square

XIV

Hang the children by
their buttons to the gate.
Arrange the chairs
as you would a hexagram or a recipe.
Send for the trees swaying
like bells about to awaken.
Nail the callouses
of your feet to the door like
a prize brought home.
Lace the wheel's spokes with yellow ribbons
and lead it like a tapestry.
Have a few books for the shelves.
In the garden, near the children,
line up the stones by sizes.
They are useless
and benign as Christmas but
you must have them.
Rechart the constellations
to complement the wallpaper.
Be careful they don't rob you
of what you never had. They are tricky,
and suicidal as New Year's Eve
but you will insist on their punctuality.
Uncrate the shadows, let them
find their own way home.
Plant the teeth in measured rows.
Then sit down and wait.
No one will come but you don't know that.

95

Poem To An Imaginary Japanese Lover

 Kotaro shall we go to a country
where language is a whistle
carved from our bones
and every face you've never known
is etched in the soft palm of your nights

I pull a plug from the moon
and watch it shrivel
they say the Japanese see in it
a rabbit pounding rice

It is necessary not to speak
of important things
It is necessary to address myself to strangers

These days follow each other like children
robbing us
or settling down to sleep
in their boxes

Kotaro shall we follow them and never rest
making love on river beds, dispelling droughts
cleaning our teeth with charcoal and salt
shall we let them take us
slowly
until we are memory
like that windbag moon
or the pocket of a ragged beggar's coat
that will not get him through the winter
96

travel until something in us
recognizes the landscape
of hands the stillplanet of our bones

HOW TO DETERMINE YOUR BIRTHDAY UPON WAKING IN A STRANGE PLACE WHICH IS MORE THAN LIKELY YOUR OWN BED   for Andrei Codrescu

XVI

Take calendars.
Take a morning, waking
and suddenly it's waking to a name
thursday
and a place
april
and a prophecy
23.
Take clocks.
Take a.m. or p.m.
Take 3.
Take 7.
In this way it is not necessary
to judge the seasons. They will come
regardless.
It matters little if you fail
to recognize the white as winter
or if you call autumn by another name.
Everything that happens happens
without you.
The years can be judged with mirrors.
Or whatever.
Give yourself a free rein.

Take the sleek landscape of your skin.
Take sorrow.
Take the clothes you wear to hide them
from the world.

Mute's Definition

it is a shell in thick beds
angry at intrusion
molding mucous like a snail
or spider
shaping the sea stone
in layers
to be worn on an ear
that won't talk back

it is the poem soft
with indecision, screaming
like a hive of bees
the poem restless like tumbleweed
scuttling across roads
in search of a garden, a voice

Blind Man's Definition

it has taken me until now
to be able to say
even this
it has taken me this long
to know what I cannot say
like the names of mutes
lost in their sticky invisible nets

wearing alphabets heavy on their chests
like ivory beads of a rosary

it is sea stones bitten
like coins, carried in pouches
to be traded for whiskey
and black-haired women
it is the poem about a spiral staircase

Deaf Man's Definition

it is a pearl, a universe of mouths
loudest at the core
that covers and covers
until its walls are deep enough
to hold the screaming in
it is the blind man's eye
it is the secret of distance
held beautifully
white histories on the ears of women
sea scrolls remaining mute and lost

it is the poem clawing its box
voiceless
shaking damp feathers
a pair of lips to be read
like a novel

XVIII ...I would have tied my breasts in a black slip
and added bells to the ribbons
I would have washed my face with white earth
and piled my hair
I would have given a scarlet streak to the parting
with a whisker of barley.

—*Uraon dance poem*

ends
era
ending
goes
so quickly
the eye cannot see
or measure it
gone
like a harvest
or migration
of birds
gone
like houses
after the fire
left from this
place
like a blindman's cane
like memory
jaded
gone like your knees
101

like your fingers
your cheeks
gone in an instant

so empty you
can see for miles

Sweet Revenge

 There are women.
The rhythm of their hips
insures the fertility of cattle.
To touch them
is to be impervious
to disease or pain.
The ground beneath their feet
is used in the curing of warts
and gallstones.
To bring rain, they are sprinkled
with water in a dance.
Since the last time I saw you
I've become
one of these women.

XX   thumb
        poet of misfortune
        who nine days dead
        lights the burglar's path
        and throws houses
        into black sleep.
        left thumb of a dead child
        for the curing of warts.

        thumb and index.
        the free man.
        the devil's saddle.

        index
        singer of good fortune.
        protector of water.
        assurance from drowning.

        middle.
        sorcerer.
        father of vampires.
        blood of the left is prophet
        of lost things.
        talisman in wood on the mourner's chest.

        finger of rings.
        digitus medicus. a red string
        will hold the sickness
        cut it from the body.
        104

little finger.
magpie.
charm of thieves.
enemy of purses.

Hannya

CAROL TINKER

struck and calm
i want what you want
a calm
empty days and
cumulative energy like thought
forgetting

Naramasu

hungry, you with
the wish   come
reach a form

i chewed wheat
embers of namelessness

the wild grass
                    the bamboo grove
the sparrows seethe.

wet green hallelujahs

casket
of leaf green
                    hallelujahs
the heart of the wait's
got singly
binderies of books
and closet queens and
anger with
                    nothing anger
settled period

as no moving
                    like hard rain
lying at the feet of the
wet green
                    hallelujahs

Heron of Oblivion

heaven declares
the heron of oblivion
thökk weeps
waterless tears
for balefire
       living or dead
       they knew him not
       the drowned boy
heron of oblivion
who slits the hearts of men

i got caught
in the hall of the heron
in a night in winter
i was snagged
i was carefully netted

half o'er
the delaware
cold flesh
in amber

my eyes dim
i cannot see
be my spectacles
the spectacle to see
the image the inscription
the baleful moon
half o'er the delaware
walter tyndall dead

112

golden triangle

i was a saint
went up in a
basket
seventy times as high
as the moon

"i saw pittsburgh
i saw town
i saw allegheny   upside down"

    saw eighty million working women
    ride red hot motorcycles
    saw many many women
    working all the time

saw a woman
eating breakfast at sunset

saw one hat
on the precise, teak

    (many, many)

hooks.

the tissue sent with
vision the integrity of
carcinoma of tons of flesh
of bones of bellies nail parings
burning in an ashtray

here's a dog
drill down
unconnected sound sending
    the frets go dark
        goldbeater's membrane

through which
    he's standing talking not me

die two at a time arbutus
smell it   a white noon
assimilate the female principle
not a
love story

it works so slow it
takes days and
then there's wet
water
the same cellar

it was pretty, what i
wanted to say
left out in it all falling
hourly the louse comb and
larkspur
and a black velvet pillow
again, again like
picking shrimp
nits in the hair
worms in the brain

aside
why attitudes
a red heart weeps
anywords   stop stop the folding water

too late

it's too late it goes
it goes faster why i wanted

why

115

a smart & final iris

sound rising
acquires a
musical structure

light falls off
by squares

     love is death
     feed the hungry ghost

     here is meet and
     fitting female
     here is flint
     harder than steel

there are celebrities
that are just like you
and just like me
and just like marsden hartley
at the second german sound shift
at the
     smart & final
          iris company
cash & carry wholesale grocery

     there searched according
     to gottweig
     interstadial custom they
     said

GRAVELLY LAKE PONDERS!
> or:
>> relax sweetie you're not going anywhere

STOP CASTING POROSITY!
> or:
>> stick with me baby
>> we'll see our names in lights

lank pier

partially
off course the moment rises
part ebbs
reflects at the lank pier
sags below the surface
tension
far too much too taut
sight it
put a beyond
a *cimaise*

set up
a decision approach
slowly
regard

the inventory round the
many axes many
decisions then
contemplate a vanishing
point a topological
change the left
hand come upon the
method juxtaposition

a monopoly an
image cluster of such
pith that any way you throw
the jackstraws of
118

changing light
at the change of axis
where the tension slacks a
cosmos immanent
set up a
decision
at the lank pier

How can we end human suffering

tired, soft
and full of blood
what am I doing in Berlin

the first hoarfrost covers the mole
yellow beech leaves falling
branches beating on my window
in West Berlin where
walls are thin
and the dogs don't shit in the streets
and war widows in fedoras eat ice cream
every day in the cafés in Wannsee
the same old American tanks roll down
                        Kronprinzenstrasse
the old man calls you to the phone
and you don't speak the language
he was a Nazi
but now he's
nice
            a truckdriver stops
            at an intersection
            to yell at Mary
            her hair too long, skirts too short
            waiting for the light to change

LEEE VEEENG TAY AHH TERR...

tonight in Berlin
the Living Theater's *Frankenstein,*

120

about
> how can we end human suffering

Pamela Badyk reads from the *New York Times:*

RACE RIOT IN SAN FRANCISCO

home

late tonight hearing
the usual guns from Tegelsee
over the last of Schinkel
a quarter mile from the Wall

I'm not talking about the trade in Zoo Station
the storing of butter for siege
the rising age of Berlin's population
the refuge for war resistors
the bombed out, productive, teeming east—

the stars tonight are remote but clear
the long acorns roll
wind lifts leaves across the driveway
at sea level on the northern plain

> Matthew Johnson, sixteen
> jumped out of the car, ran
> Alvin Johnson in middle age shot him

> San Francisco's hills
> are higher than Sydney harbor's
> the flats of Hunters Point are black
> the valley of Fillmore Hill is black

in came the Po Leece
in came your friend the sergeant
the sheriff, the deputies, the highway patrol
the national guard, the reserves
the mayor

Jack Shelley came down
from Diamond Heights to Hunters Point
I've spent my life with the unions
I am a union man
the trouble is the unions
they don't do all they can

I believe in
the North Sea. It is wet.
There are people on top
and a lot under.

the new moon this november
33 year cycle of Leonids
can't be seen over Berlin
the ceiling is low and troubled over Europe
water sweeps Italy
flooding Florence
water challenges London
heavy seas take the long coasts

no Leonids for you tonight
the guns from Tegelsee
and wind on Wannsee
keep you from sleeping

in violet light a white sun
a strange mother threw a wormy litter
122

old feet in the Pacific   clam hunters in November
the grunion filled Cold Mountain Cove
then there is pigeon blood on the luckystone
and sourgrass that can't be eaten
someone is fishing in the dry Tehachapis
fragrant in the knowledge of the love of God

cool undersea freshwater sources show up darker

living on the corner of Dog and Shit
in the Wobbly City
on the San Andreas Fault
sitting in the death seat
ain't like living in sin
sitting in the mudflats of South Basin
sitting in

to teach you
they make you do it over
                              and over
you'll learn

the word for it is:

fires in the night
rifle shots
broken bottles on the doorstep
the sound truck and the skunk car
Shabazz the con man and Tom from SNCC
meet the door to door acid salesman
and loose a specter
the hungry I & Thou
and the world cheered
        put out candles with spit

123

                    advancing hourly down
                                Kronprinzenstrasse

yelling
        DON'T FUCK WITH THEM:
                                KILL THEM

if you cannot learn this language
this is for you.

XI   "The bitter wormwood shivers in the endless plains"
Benedict the Pole was sustained by Ovid
in Baluchistan
dryland flushed by mirage—
      this land of continuous riding
      I pray to God that I may be relieved
cut off my hand
tear out my tongue
scratch out my eyes

      flying eastward toward war

                        Kabul

125

Shiva
is dancing
in the fire
as you turn those pages

as you turn those pages
fine paper ashes float
through the room
your voice drones on

those marching in the streets
have fired the garbage on the stairs
and throw flaming papers in the air
ashes drift and swirl
around your head

as you turn those pages
each weft of the cloth
of your clothes
holds a
pulsing
star

yes, sam johnson,

    "prodigious noble wild prospects"

but christ
i feel like ned kelly
looking down from
buena vista heights
on the city—

    frisco in the lotus
    your pluck hung high
    your veins opened

    the halitus of haight street
    rises with incense
    this cold morning

person who stole
landlady's wash left her
without panties stockings bathtowels
her blue housedress is gone too

must have been poor and ornery
and her size

fine yachts in the harbor
make a difference between
the law of inventory
and the right to
lynch

> handles riveted to the leather satchel
> and grain of golden oak
> this is not a quiet night
> guns and sirens and running feet
> screeching tires screams
> breaking glass and more shots, this
> time an automatic rifle

read this for its sentiment
differentiating lynch law from
the right to inventory

buddha's birthday
     in memory of martin luther king, jr.

come & see   you
have shown me
passion

wind blows the eucalypts
and sun shines through
in the panhandle
prime among others
              my moving eye

april the fourth month
new spring gardens:
dogwood flowers on lower market street

buddha's birthday

requiem mass for brother martin
we circumambulate the cathedral and the
                   pacific union club

passover
      easter

or in the revelation of john:

      nevertheless i have somewhat against thee
      because thou hast left thy first love

129

the venerable bede
knew of the wolf
taught his paternoster
by monks
all he could say
was lamb,
                    lamb

sunday parlor park freeway

XVI   the legs of the piano
stool are clawing glass
balls eating
everyone's spaghetti

bang bang
        within the exact length of time
                         of the explosion

everyone stabbed the sleeping bag
kapok blooming
        on the star thistle

your mail is late
your health didn't get here
your health is missing
that   is   it   has
been discovered as missing ruby
throated hummingbird in the bottlebrush tree
hummingbird prefers the red memo
germans prefer the hummingbird
and a
        personal squirrel

                (i'll watch the kid lady)

the cars are dividing and reproducing like the greedy
        cancer cells in the film

131

and there's only three feet eight inches
between us and them

it is not mucilege it is white glue
it is not casein it is commercial epoxy
        with a fiberglass body

        pogrom sam secret anarchist
used cars san bernardino
if you happen to catch his eye you might
be surprised to hear of his
completely worked out escape route:

through canada to ireland to norway

my dear   we remove   to a seashore life

he is gay too and
interested in australian mines
all this money and
no ideas

thank you capitalism
for the expanding universe

XVII   o tucumcari lady took good care of you
tucumcari lady made you free
roast dog and fat tobacco tea

says
i'm better than a restaurant
comforted with scalpels, peeling
off a billboard
laughing in the stretcher
happy in the bread machine
       reclaimed from greyhound

pure mind knows
she broke you
of riots and spreading diseases
so that all your clothes are washed forever
so that you could stand here naked

cellists!   pomos!   fleas!
mary pestered by angels!
hermes nude on washday his finger in the dyke!

it is hard   *it is duty*

tucumcari took good care of you
it's just that history
got you busted

Zuni ring knocks
against steel
wheelbarrow
uneven bricks   room of bronze
tree
        color of brains
        color of pulse

inordinate bloom
mimosa underfoot
and that foot
bare and calloused
that dry sky with a sea haze
begging crows on the three legged ladder

134

I watch cypress
trees through the smoke
of the fire

I watch their trunks seethe and shiver
and everything i can see through the smoke
seethes and shivers the same way

and I am seized again with shameless talk
and you so sick with suffering

Ishtar
or the explosion in a shingle factory

growing
        growing
i'm gagging on jelly
doughnuts full of nitroglycerine
to steady the heart
which is in a peculiar spasm

i've got apples and
you don't

my hand covers the characters and
smears them as i write and
i write large now
to make something of myself
fingernail parings, flaking skin,
hair combings
dry dead cells settle from the air
faded but without blemish

they wanted to know if it's poetry
or is it a black flag

boys see more dead cats
than girls; write
bloodier letters

hard brown sugar sticks
in the bowl
i mean i'm trying to
claw it out with this
menorah of burning fingers

a thousand miles not a single
stoplight no books a slow
disentanglement of weeds

rain on the roof
a thousand heavy dancing crows

a high ditched road through fields of milo

a thousand miles and no stoplight
rain raining so hard and so often

this layer of atmosphere close to the ground
is water, a lucid fog
and the small leaves of the live oak,
cotoneaster, acacia, mimosa
shine with a wet shine
and move with the motion
of a thousand miles
a thousand crows

from Hannya

 they have reached
me their eyes are bright
where are you whose eyes are lights in trouble
they walk out to see and are seen in the light of their walking
and so the stars shine
waxing or waning according to the vision fixed on them
their eyes
interrogate
the quick of question
inquest and conscience
artifacts of the future past
your single retreat
repeats
you have done
near your heart
in the mountain's merciless beauty
removed therefrom
from love to terror
to the bright will's inquest
removed to a justice
like no other justice
your own two eyes slay me suddenly
i may the beauty of them not sustain
so woundeth they me
terror not sustain
mercilessness not sustain
in fire
consumed in silence
in

death of spirit
waste of shame
world hysterical
world without end
noise in silence
silence in company
eyes that like it

thin
comes hard rain
strong sweated thin
in the flux of ashes
in the thin air
thin song in the hours of death

no no later
no now and no later

eternal vigilantes price
preservation to dissolve
from supersaturated organisms
small rain

danger is to you
as you are to will
and always one plane binding the spectra
the colors of distant carbons
the cataracts in eyes
standing looking standing
turning all colors infra red
fact

light seen looking upward underwater
light on water

140

light passing through water
in an instant   to apperceive an instant

i did not seem to be buying
or enduring
returns
of priming by sea
of primitive accumulation
of constant capital
and enduring the wearing
backwash of locked up surplus
princedoms and powers
until this morning lying in bed
through the curtains the glare
of sea light in high rooms
cold ribcage called cathedral
a day and a night in a house
poised in air
dangerous purchase
a feint in air
this is a situation fraught with danger
it's called making
a living out of
things

the cloud ring
the blind spot of the eye
conspire the death you want

no reciprocal, they move
from room to room
or sleep alone unstalked
but the loneliness takes the personality of
him, that is lonely, is evil

141

you can will anything
to speak in twos, each to each
as though in a courtroom
veer toward each other and turn away
you can come and go
but
water
turns and
flows through the universe
turns as you turn
into itself and vanishes

fasting fasting from walls and jambs
from senses you use wholly
in mind alone
sleeping alone

it had been going on for hours
the room has been going on for hours
as no other room
and less a hunger
the side of the form
creates itself
going on for hours
air moves wind blows
shiver wake
the voices stop
they stop
when wind blows air moves because
no later
the rapids silting up
the sacred empty faces
that are familiar
that are yours

in the false space of future documents
leaves wet feet grass stains
loud and sacred

one-eyed odin sees
through scar tissue infra red
sees the cloud ring the blind spot
the eyes that called
the bloody muster

from The Young Emerald, Evening Star

XXIII   as light goes
it pierces the river
where the rogue river enters the pacific
i sit on a salted log
in white sand   in wild phlox
i think of you who thinks of a woman
secret and hungry

light into mixing waters   sky and ocean meet
                the color of solder
sheep graze the sea meadow
glow above the moving waters
a tongue in a throat sings
to the evening star
white and black and green at sunset
august 1966: now the platonists said
souls come through cancer
and leave through capricorn

what i am i lay before you
the person
thinking on person
thinking on these things
light is going into water

the north wind shows
silver of poplar and beech
you are not rock
buried in the mountain

144

along the valley of the skagit to the ocean
are islands orcas and lummi
at the end of a drained
valley full of dutch and
odd steeples   overhead lightning
get the door open
you are not rock   you are alone

fern in ditch
salmon and cod
brine and sweetwater meet
night hawks over bellingham never stop crying

south wind brings rain
north from serpentine and redwoods
to vancouver sound
where over down timber logs are driven
        go from the known to the known
        taxonomy
        go from the known to the known
        volition
go from these
        rather than these
there is other

Biographical Notes

JESSICA TARAHATA HAGEDORN (b. 1949, Manila, the Philippines), arrived in San Francisco in 1962 and has worked in films, music and theater. An editor of the forthcoming anthology of literature and graphics, *Third World Women*, to be published by the Third World Communications Collective, she is presently working on a one-act play. *Chiquita Banana*, evoking Carmen Miranda, to be included in the anthology. She is also the author of the widely circulated but as yet unpublished erotic, picaresque tale, *Pet Food*.

ALICE KARLE was born April 17, 1949, in New York City and grew up in Long Beach, New York. She spent most of the next five years in Isla Vista attending UCSB with her dog, Thor. She was graduated in Religious Studies. She is the author and the editor of *Figs* (Red Sky Press), illustrated by Christopher Tong, publisher of *Four Dog Mountain Songs*, Doggerel Press, 1972.

BARBARA SZERLIP (b. 1949, New Jersey), attended the University of Miami and UCSB. She has lived and traveled extensively in Mexico, worked in theater in New York State and spent some time at the Sivananda Yoga Ashram, Quebec, as a cook and instructor in hatha-yoga and kurtan mantras. The author of *Teopantiahuac*, Walter Table Press, her work has appeared in *The North Stone Review, Heirs, Another Poetry Magazine* and *Spectrum*. She is the editor of *Tractor*, a poetry magazine published in San Francisco, where she now lives.

CAROL TINKER (b. 1940, Pittsburgh, Pennsylvania), bears the surname of the tribes of traveling metallurgists that the Greeks called Chalybes. One of three children, she grew up in Pennsylvania, New York, Japan and Brandywine Hundred, Delaware, before attending Carnegie Mellon University. A painter and poet, she moved to San Francisco in 1962, did some theater work, was active in community defense in the Haight Ashbury and in 1966 initiated what became the Artists' Liberation Front (alias the Empire Cement Company). She traveled around the world in 1966–1967 and now lives in Santa Barbara; some of her poems have appeared in *The Beloit Poetry Journal, Intransit, Upriver,* Barbara Szerlip's *Tractor*, and *New Directions 26.* A hannya is a Japanese female demon that comes to life from a moment of overpowering hatred of one person for another.